GOOD

OLD-FASHIONED
ADVICE

First published in Great Britain in 2005 by Robson Books, The Chrysalis Building,
Bramley Road, London W10 6SP

An imprint of Chrysalis Books Group plc

First published in 2004 by Gusto Company AS
Copyright © 2004, 2005 Gusto Company AS

British Library Cataloguing in Publication Data
A catalogue for this title is available from the British Library

ISBN1 86105 867 5

Original concept by James Tavendale and Ernesto Gremese
Illustrated by Greg Paprocki, Artville and Photodisc
Original design by Chili Design AS
Original Cover Design by SEE Design
Printed by SNP Leefung, China

GOOD

OLD-FASHIONED
ADVICE

By Michael Powell

Introduction

What is the best advice you have ever heard, and more importantly, what is the best advice you have ever taken?

Advice generally takes two forms: it tells us to do things or to avoid them. People have been giving and taking it for thousands of years, and it's amazing that so much of this stuff has percolated down to future generations.

In this book I have gathered together a whole heap of ancient lore. It forms a timeworn though timely oasis, where those of us who are baffled by the bustling and brooding impatience of contemporary life can take stock and soak up a few abiding axioms, even glean a few timeless truths.

Some of the advice we can attribute to last Tuesday and some can be traced to folk who lived long before the pyramids were built. But good advice is timeless. All it needs is a place, a time and an ear willing to listen.

A few years ago, a truck driver friend of mine was driving across the American Midwest. He had been on the road for hours and was dead beat, hungry and in need of a little human company. In the small hours he pulled over and parked outside a small all-night diner. After taking a seat, the waitress came to take his order. He said "I would like ham, fried eggs over easy, hash browns, tomatoes, two slices of hot buttered toast and some kind words."

A few minutes later the waitress returned with his order, placed it in front of him and turned to leave. "Hang on, ma'am", said my friend, "You've forgotten something – what about those words of kindness?"

Hands on hips, the waitress stared at him for a moment. Then leaning in so close that only he could hear, she whispered, "Don't eat them eggs".

Michael Powell

Contents

CHAPTER 1

Travelling Tips

Throw a shoe over the roof of your house and whichever way the toe is pointing when it lands indicates the direction in which you will soon be travelling.

Put ferns in your shoes if you want to find treasure.

It is unlucky to begin a cruise on a Friday (the day when Christ died) or the second Monday in August (when Sodom and Gomorrah were destroyed).

Be wary of travelling on a Monday.

On your travels, to meet someone with flat feet brings bad luck.

When you hear the first cuckoo of the year, whichever direction you are facing is the way you will find yourself travelling before the end of the year.

When reading tea leaves, a straight line of leaves indicates that you will make a journey; an arch suggests that this journey will be abroad.

Turning in the direction of your house once you have left it is bad luck, so turning round and waving should be avoided. If you have left something behind, it is better to continue your journey rather than go back for it. If you really must return, sit down and count to ten before resuming your trip.

THROWING SHOES AFTER SOMEONE WHO IS LEAVING ON A JOURNEY WILL BRING THEM GOOD LUCK.

When waving a person goodbye, it is unlucky to watch them disappear from sight, as this signifies that you will never see them again.

If there is a funeral in your vicinity, do not leave the town or travel far until it is over, otherwise your trip will be inauspicious.

If you meet a woman with red hair on your travels, you must go home and begin your journey all over again, unless you wish to be cursed with the pangs of labour pains.

When you are being chased by a ghost, climb through the cleft of a tree to confuse the spirit and help you to escape.

Always leave a house by the same door by which you entered.

A sick man on board a ship will not die until land has been sighted.

Do not count the carriages of a passenger train or you will hear news of a death.

CHAPTER 2

Babies
and
Pregnancy

If You Want a Girl ...

- Make love in the afternoon.
- Ensure the woman orgasms first.
- The woman should initiate sex.
- Make love on even days of the month.
- You should both eat lots of fish and vegetables.
- Make love with the woman on top.
- Eat chocolate and other sweets.
- Make love under a full moon.
- Go horse riding.
- Use the missionary position.

If You Want a Boy ...

- Make love at night.
- Eat lots of red meat.
- Make love on odd days of the month.
- Eat salty snacks.
- Men must have lots of fizzy drinks.
- Lying down after sex gives the boy sperm a chance to beat the girl sperm to the egg.
- Make love standing up.
- Try the rear-entry position.
- The woman should sleep on the left.
- Make love with the woman's head pointing north.

During pregnancy

If the mother's left breast is bigger than the right it's a girl. If the right is bigger, it's a boy. If they are the same size, who knows?

If her age at conception and the year of conception are both even or both odd, the baby is a girl. If one is even and one is odd, the baby is a boy.

Suspend a gold ring on a chain over the mother's palm. If the ring moves in

a circular motion, it will be a girl. If it swings back and forth it indicates a boy.

If the mother carries the baby forwards (her bump is invisible from behind) she will have a boy. If she carries the baby sideways (her bump is visible from behind) she will have a girl.

When the mother picks up a key, if she picks it up by the round end, it will be a boy. If she picks it up by the long end, it will be a girl. If she picks it up at the middle, she will have twins.

If the mother likes to rest on her left side, it's a boy; on her right, it's a girl.

When the mother shows you her hands, if they are palms up, it's a girl; palms down, a boy.

CHAPTER 3

Business Etiquette

When making small talk, stick to neutral topics that won't offend. It is a chance to find common ground, so agree with what others are saying. If not, change the subject. Do not talk about yourself but make comments that are relevant to the current situation. Avoid being too flippant, otherwise you may damage your credibility.

People like and identify with those who appear to be most like them. Mirror the body language and vocal patterns of others; try to match their tone, rhythm and speed of speaking while maintaining an open and welcoming posture.

Honesty in business, as in life, pays dividends. Sincerity is the best way to win trust, clients and customers. Quality is the second most important thing, but the trust must come first. Fast and cheap always loses faith in the long term.

When shaking hands, stand up, look the other person in the eye and grip their hand firmly. Smile. Make sure the crook of your finger and thumb meets theirs. Shake crisply up and down and say 'Pleased to meet you'. Release hands while maintaining eye contact. Listen to their name rather than thinking about how you may appear to them. Then try to use it during the next sentence. This will help to fix it in your memory.

The customer really is always right. An unsatisfied customer tells his friends – your potential customers. Treat a customer as a valued member of your family. If your focus isn't with the customer, shift it until it is.

In business, all good things take time. Growing your business is the bottom line. Make a plan and stick to it. Grow your business slowly and be flexible.

ALWAYS ARRIVE ON TIME, EVEN IF YOU KNOW THAT THE OTHER PARTY ALWAYS KEEPS YOU WAITING.

Do not take a phone call when you are with a client unless it is to say "I am with a client, please may I call you back in one hour".

A timely 'thank you' can give you advantage in all sort of business situations. In marketing it offers a subtle reminder to your customers that you can be called upon again the next time they wish to do business. It's a polite way of asking and giving at the same time.

If you aren't passionate about your business, find another business.

CHAPTER 4

Decorative Napkin Folding

It would be possible to write an entire book on this subject, so here are three ideas to add a touch of sophistication to your entertaining.

1. Simple Pyramid

With a corner facing you, fold the napkin in half diagonally away from you. Then fold the two bottom corners of the triangle into the top corner. Turn it over and fold diagonally in half away from you again. Now stand it up on the table.

2. Bishop's Hat

With a corner facing you, fold the napkin in half diagonally away from you. Then fold the two bottom corners of the triangle into the top corner.

- Fold the bottom corner three quarters of the way towards the top corner.
- Fold the top front corner down to meet the bottom edge.
- Fold the top flaps down and tuck them under the front fold.
- Turn the napkin over and fold one corner under the other so that it can stand up on the table.

3. Glass Lily

- Fold the napkin in half twice to form a small square.
- Concertina and repeat on the other side.
- Place the napkin upright in a wine glass and spread out the petals.

CHAPTER 5

Flower Arranging

Before you begin, make a mental picture of how you want your arrangement to look and pay careful attention to where it will be displayed when it is complete.

If you are using foam, choose the right type – green water-retaining foam for fresh flowers and brown foam for dried flowers. Ensure the green foam is well soaked in a bucket or bowl (rather than under a tap which is less effective) for about 20 seconds. Over-soaking will make the foam disintegrate.

Cut stems with a sharp knife or pair of scissors at a 45-degree angle. This will allow water to enter the stems and your arrangement will last longer. Never break the stems with your fingers. A jagged edge prevents water absorption.

First lay down the flowers that create the basic 'shape' of the piece. If the arrangement doesn't work out, it is often the fault of the first five flowers that you placed.

Work with a variety of colours, shapes, sizes and textures. Use straight leaves and flowers to create the outline shape, rounded flowers for focus and fuller flowers to link them together. Balance colours, so that one part does not dominate another.

Generally the flowers at the bottom of the arrangement are the darkest and the lightest flowers go at the top and edges.

Mix flowers in bud with those half open and in full bloom. Buds should go at the top and edges of the arrangement and the largest flowers should be in the centre and towards the bottom. Large flowers that are too high make an arrangement look top heavy.

Each flower should have its own space. Crowding flowers together is unnatural and distracting (when do you see flowers touching in nature?)

Do not face all your flowers forward; turn some of them at different angles.

Be aware of the smells of the flowers. A strong-smelling arrangement in a small room can be overpowering. The smell of flowers on a dinner table should never dominate the meal.

Go with your gut feeling rather than stick with the 'rules'. Do what pleases your eye rather than what the experts tell you. Personal expression is more important than a rigid set of dos and don'ts.

BE AWARE OF THE SMELLS OF THE FLOWERS.

CHAPTER 6

Golf Etiquette

There's more to golf than hitting a ball into a hole and trying to stay out of the water and the bunkers. There are centuries of tradition and etiquette to consider.

Don't take swings (even practice swings) when there is someone in front of you. It is bad manners and dangerous, as you might hit stones and bits of turf towards them.

Keep the noise down, especially when someone else is taking a shot. A noisy group or individual is a distraction to other players. Treat the green like a library.

Don't waste too much time searching for a lost ball as it holds up play for your group and those behind you.

Never run. Always walk. If you need to go fast, walk fast but lightly, or drive your golf cart at a moderate speed. Anything else is distracting and risks damaging the course.

Maintain a good pace of play and keep up with those ahead of you so that you don't hold up those behind. Even taking 15 seconds less time between shots can shave half an hour off your round time. Plan your shot while others are taking their turn (e.g. choice of club).

If your shot throws up a divot (a small lump of turf and soil) from the ground, always tidy up after you; put it back where it came from and lightly firm it down with your foot.

Always enter a bunker from the low side nearest your ball. Do not climb in from the top, as this will damage the wall. After your shot, use the rake to erase your footprints. Leave the rake outside the bunker with the handle pointing in the same direction as the fairway.

In a bunker you are not allowed to test the sand, either by picking it up or touching it with your club. The only time your club may touch the sand is during your stroke.

On the green, do not step on the imaginary line between someone else's ball and the hole, as you could cause a dent in the ground and destroy their chances of making a clean putt. Walk behind balls or step over the line.

Mark up your scores on the way to the next tee, not on the green. Always leave the green as soon as your group has finished.

Use your ball mark repair tool to repair the mark that your ball made when it landed on the green.

CHAPTER 7

Good Luck

Here are 50 ways to have good luck:

- Sneeze three times before breakfast.
- Meet three sheep.
- Look at the new moon over your right shoulder.
- Find a four-leafed clover.
- Carry a rabbit's foot.
- Find a horseshoe.
- Wear your clothes inside out.
- Wear your birthstone.
- Blow out all your candles on your birthday cake with a single breath.
- Find a cricket in your house.
- Find a penny heads up.
- See a spider spinning in the morning.
- Carry an acorn – it brings long life as well as good luck.
- A robin flies into your house.
- A frog enters your house.
- Cut your hair during a storm.
- Avoid stepping on cracks in the pavement.
- Accept a sprig of white heather from a gypsy.
- Get an itch on top of your head.
- A ladybird lands on you.
- Pick up a piece of coal that has fallen in your path.
- Catch your clothes on a thorn bush.
- Begin a new project on a new moon.
- Dolphins swim close to your ship.
- Have luck on the golf course by having an odd number of clubs and balls with numbers less than four.
- Shake hands with a chimney sweep.
- On the first day of the month make sure 'white rabbits' is the first thing you say after waking.
- The first butterfly you see in the year is white.
- Carry a badger's tooth (especially if you are a gambler).
- Meet a goat during an important journey.
- Carry an oyster shell.

FIND A
PENNY
HEADS UP.

24

Sleep facing south.

- Wind up all the clocks in your house as soon as the New Year begins.
- Eat black-eyed peas on New Year's Day.
- Spit in your hand before picking up a baseball bat.
- Spit on your bait before casting your fishing rod.
- To win a hockey match, tap the goalie on his shin pads before the game.
- Pick up a pin.
- Bring a cat on board ship.
- See two crows.
- Hang a picture of an elephant facing the door.
- Have a high instep.
- Play golf in the rain.
- If you are a bride it is good luck if you meet any of the following: a lamb, spider, dove, policeman, blind man, black cat, clergyman.
- A child cries during your wedding ceremony.
- Women: wear yellow underwear on New Year's Eve.
- After you've eaten a boiled egg, push the spoon through the bottom of the shell to allow the devil to escape.
- Always shave before taking part in a rodeo competition.
- Spill wine while proposing a toast.
- See a shooting star.

CHAPTER 8

Home Remedies

Bee stings

Dab with lemon juice and apply a paste of baking soda and water.

Cut a green onion and hold it on the sting to relieve the pain.

Hold a banana peel on the sting.

Bubonic plague
To protect yourself from Bubonic plague, wear a spider in a walnut shell around your neck.

Chapped lips or hands
Apply glycerine and lemon juice in equal amounts and leave overnight.

Cuts

Raw honey has been used for centuries to prevent and heal infection. Apply raw honey and cover with a bandage. The pain from a small cut should disappear after half an hour, but you can leave the dressing on overnight.

Headache

Place equal parts of natural apple cider vinegar and water in a pan and bring to the boil. Inhale the fumes for about 60 breaths.

Hiccups

Swallow a teaspoon of vinegar.

Plug your ears with your fingers and drink through a straw.

Sunburn

Whip an egg white and beat in a teaspoon of castor oil. Apply to the affected areas.

Add a handful of baking soda to your warm bath.

Throat infection

Tie a wolf's right paw around your neck.

Warts

Peel the skin thinly off a potato and rub the potato side on the wart three times a day. In two weeks the wart will turn black and drop off.

Rub a frog on your wart. If you don't have a frog handy, then rub the wart with a peeled apple and give it to a pig.

Worms

To cure yourself of worms, eat horse-hairs chopped finely in between two slices of bread and butter.

CHAPTER 9

How to Eat Sushi

Before the meal your waitress will bring you a hot towel called an oshibori. Use it to wipe your hands before eating. Do not mop your brow or clean your face with it.

With your sushi order, you will receive a portion of pickled ginger and a small mound of wasabi. The ginger acts as a palate cleanser between various sushi dishes. Mix the wasabi with the soy sauce depending on how spicy you like it. Careful though – wasabi is very hot.

You may use your fingers or chopsticks to eat your food.

If taking food from a shared plate, use the reverse ends of your chopsticks rather than the ends which go in your mouth.

Do not dip chopsticks vertically into food, especially into a bowl of rice. Never use your chopsticks to pass food. Pass the plate instead.

Don't bite into a piece of food and then put the remainder on your plate. You should eat whatever you pick up in one mouthful.

When not eating, place your chopsticks in front of you, parallel to the edge of the sushi bar, with the eating ends in the hashi oki (a small ceramic block); don't place them directly on the bar.

Leaving food is considered rude, but especially rice. Never leave rice.

Do not smoke in a sushi bar, even if there is an ashtray provided (as is common in many Western sushi bars). Smoke will obscure the subtle flavours of the fish for everyone, including you.

Dip the sushi in the soy with the rice side up. The soy is supposed to flavour the fish, not the rice, so using the rice to soak up the soy by dipping the sushi rice side down is wrong. It also makes the sushi fall apart.

Eat sushi slowly. Great care and time is taken in its preparation and so you should show great discernment when you eat it to fully enjoy both the taste and the texture.

CHAPTER 10

How to make a Perfect Cup of Tea

Follow these instructions to ensure that your tea is perfect every time:

Use cold water that has been freshly drawn from the tap, or even better, filtered.

Use a kettle that is free from dirt or limescale.

Use a ceramic teapot and heat it first with some of the hot water from the kettle before adding the tea leaves.

Avoid tea bags. Loose tea makes the best brew – one teaspoon per person plus one for the pot.

As soon as the water starts to boil, pour it into the tea pot. Allowing the water to boil for longer destroys oxygen and makes the water taste less fresh.

Stir and leave to brew for between three and five minutes (depending on the size of the tea leaves – the larger the leaves the longer the brewing time). If you want stronger tea, add more leaves, do not extend the brewing time, as the tea will become steeped (stewed).

Use a bone china tea cup.

Add milk to the cup and then pour in the tea, not vice versa.

Beware:
If you accidentally leave the lid off the pot, a stranger will call at your house.

It is very bad luck to forget to add the tea to the pot.

ADD MILK
TO THE CUP
AND THEN
POUR IN
THE TEA,
NOT VICE
VERSA.

When two women pour from the same teapot, one of them will become pregnant.

If you make tea that is too weak, you will fall out with a close friend; if the tea is too strong you will make a new friend.

When bubbles float on the top of your tea, if you can lift them in a teaspoon and place them in your mouth, before they touch the sides of the cup or the spoon, you will receive a letter the following morning.

Floating bubbles mean that you will become rich. If the bubbles stick to the side of the cup you will fall in love. Each bubble represents a kiss.

If two spoons are accidentally placed on the same saucer, a wedding will take place soon.

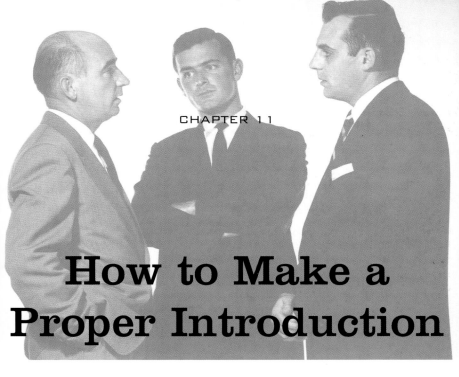

CHAPTER 11

How to Make a Proper Introduction

Making introductions is very straightforward as long as you follow a few simple rules. The key is to be aware of the status of those whom you are introducing.

When introducing people use the first and last names: "Jane Doe, I'd like you to meet Joe Bloggs" or "Jane Doe, I'd like to introduce you to Joe Bloggs."

Always include a person's title or relationship to you (e.g. Dr Black, Judge Brown, my boss, wife, brother, etc.).

Talk to the person with higher status first, e.g.
"Judge Brown, I'd like you to meet Peter Black. Peter
Black, this is Judge Brown."

When introducing a man and woman of equal status,
speak to the woman first: "Jane Pink, I'd like you to
meet Peter Black. Peter Black, this is Jane Pink."

Only introduce the woman to the man if the man is
much older or of higher status: "President Brown, I'd
like you to meet Jane Pink. Jane Pink, this is
President Brown" or "Gerald Pensioner, I'd like you to
meet Dr Jane Pink . . ."

If you are introducing a client to someone of high
status in your company, it is courteous to treat the
client as the person with the highest status, so s/he
should be addressed first: "John Client, I'd like you to
meet my boss, Sir James Important . . ."

Introduce the individual to the group first: "David
Blue, I'd like you to meet my business colleagues: Mr
James Brown, Dr Harry Orange and Katherine
Green. Everyone, this is David Blue."

If you forget someone's name it is better to apologise
and politely admit that it has slipped your mind
rather than avoid making an introduction.

If the host does not introduce you, feel free to introduce yourself to others, explaining your relationship
to the host (it immediately gives you something in
common and defers to the host).

If you think that two people have something in common, you may choose to point it out, but consider
that this may also put them on the spot and force
them to launch into a discussion of the supposed
common link, which may preclude other more inter-
esting or varied topics of conversation.

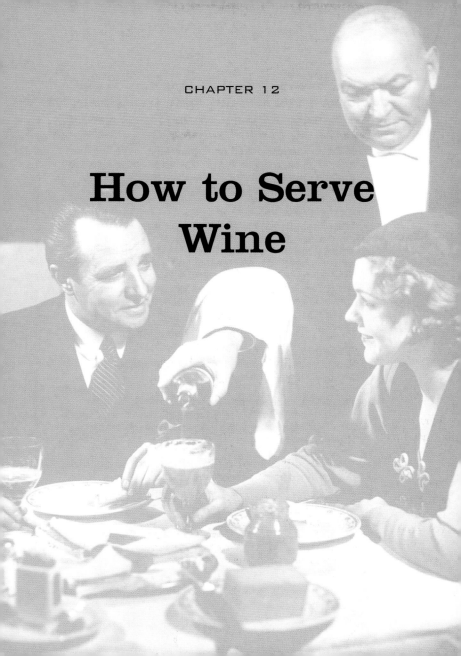

CHAPTER 12

How to Serve Wine

The two most important factors to consider when drinking wine are its temperature and the glasses it is served in.

Most people know that as a general rule white wine should be served cold and red wine at room temperature but there's more to it than this crude rule of thumb.

Temperature
Wine must be served at the correct temperature to experience its fullest flavours. Most people serve white wine too cold. Most, but not all whites, should be at 45 °F (7 °C). Any colder and you'll kill the delicate flavours and aromas. Full-bodied good quality whites such as Sauternes and Burgundies and light reds such as Beaujolais should be slightly warmer at 50°F (10 °C). Most reds should be served at 60 °F (15 °C).

Glasses
When glasses are used correctly they enhance the aromas, taste, colour and temperature.

Sparkling wines should be served in tall, tapered flutes to ensure that the bubbles stay fresh and lively. Straight glasses or wine glasses allow too many of the bubbles to escape.

White wine should be served in an 8–14oz glass, filled only to a third of its capacity, to allow the aromas to concentrate in the rim, which should curve inwards.

Red wine glasses are larger than white, between 10–16oz in size, with a round bowl that curves inwards at the top.

Avoid using coloured glasses which distort the colour of the wine – an important part of its character.

Use thin glasses, as thick ones affect the temperature of the wine. A thin glass feels crisper when it touches your lips and prepares your palate for a rich taste experience.

Ensure that your wine glasses are rinsed thoroughly and dried before use. Any trace of detergent will destroy your enjoyment.

Always hold the glass by the stem, to avoid affecting the temperature of the wine.

AVOID USING
COLOURED
GLASSES
WHICH
DISTORT THE
COLOUR OF
THE WINE

CHAPTER 13

How to Use Chopsticks

Chopsticks are traditionally used in China, Japan, Korea and Vietnam. They are made of wood, bone, ivory or plastic.

Hold chopsticks at the end (not the middle). Rest the top half of one chopstick between the thumb and forefinger of your right hand (or left if you are left handed). This chopstick does not move. Grip the other chopstick between thumb and first two fingers, the same way you would hold a pencil – move this chopstick up and down while keeping the first one fixed.

Make sure that you keep the chopsticks the same length, so that the tips can meet, otherwise you will find it very difficult to pick up food. Keep your hands relaxed. If your hand begins to ache you are too tense.

When using cheap wooden chopsticks, rub them together to remove splinters. Do not do this with more expensive sticks or you will insult your hosts.

Do not leave your chopsticks standing upright in a bowl of food (e.g. rice) as this is very unlucky and bad manners.

When taking food from a communal plate, use the thick end, which hasn't been in your mouth to transfer it to your plate (not to your mouth).

When not eating, place your chopsticks on the rest with the tips pointing left. Do not let them cross. Do not gesticulate or point at anyone else with your chopsticks.

Do not lower your head to the food; instead lift up the bowl to bring it closer to your mouth.

Do not pass food from your chopsticks to those of another person – this is associated with funerals (the bones of the deceased person are passed using chopsticks).

Do not spear food. To cut it, use a scissor action by gripping the piece very firmly between the tips, then rub the tips together sideways.

Do not dig around in a communal dish looking for the best morsels – choose food from the top, otherwise you will appear greedy.

Do not lick or suck the ends.

#

DO NOT LOWER YOUR HEAD TO THE FOOD

CHAPTER 14

Money Saving Secrets

Find a penny and pick it up and all day long you'll have good luck. If it is face down, turn it over and leave it on the floor for someone else to find.

If you steal from the dead they will come back to haunt you until you have returned what is rightfully theirs.

When you dream of manure, it is a sign that you will come into money.

When your right arm itches it is a sign that good fortune is round the corner. If your left palm is itching, you will soon have to pay out.

Remember that the Bible has been misquoted. It does not say that money is the root of evil but, "The love of money is the root of all evil". (1 Timothy 6:10)

Don't waste money on expensive wrapping paper. A roll of brightly coloured end-of-line wallpaper is ten metres long and very cheap. Even brown paper grocery bags can have a simple charm when decorated with coloured ribbon, or even tied with coarse string.

Never leave your house on an empty stomach and you won't be tempted to visit an eatery to waste half a week's grocery money on a meal. Always do your food shopping after a hearty meal.

Cut up last year's Christmas cards and send them as postcards the following year. Save on tree decorations by making popcorn chains, the old fashioned way.

Whenever you see something in the shops you must have, go home and put the money in a jar. If you still want it in a week later, take it out of the jar and buy

"THE LOVE OF MONEY IS THE ROOT OF ALL EVIL"

41

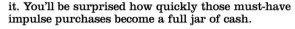

it. You'll be surprised how quickly those must-have impulse purchases become a full jar of cash.

NOBODY
EVER GOT
RICH FROM
DOING
SOMETHING
THEY
DIDN'T
LIKE.

Give up eating meat for a month. You will slash your grocery bill and reap the health benefits at the same time.

If you get a raise put the extra money into savings. An extra three per cent won't improve your quality of life, but it will boost your retirement nest egg.

Cancel cable TV for six months and play board games, listen to the wireless, read a book and talk instead. You will save money and have fun with those you love.

If you have a hobby, turn it into a money spinner. Nobody ever got rich from doing something they didn't like.

If you have a partner, budget together, rather than one of you taking care of the accounts, otherwise you won't be on the same wavelength and resentment may build up as the one 'in charge' dictates to the other what they can and can't spend.

Don't discuss your financial worries in front of your children or they will grow up sharing your insecurities about money.

CHAPTER 15

Removing stains

Ballpoint pen ink

Use methylated spirit or rub with white toothpaste, leave for five minutes and wash out.

Blood

Soak a fresh bloodstain in cold salted water; soak a dried bloodstain for several hours in a solution of one dessertspoon of ammonia to half a litre of water, then wash.

Coffee, chocolate or cocoa

Wash with a little lukewarm soapy water. Rub glycerine into the stain, leave one hour and wash again with soapy water.

Chewing Gum
Scrape away as much as possible first. Rubbing the stain with ice will harden the gum and make this easier, especially on rugs and other heavy materials. If the material is washable, soak in kerosene and wash in hot soapy water. For unwashable articles, use dry cleaning fluid.

Deodorant
Sponge the area with white vinegar and wash in the hottest water that is safe for the fabric.

Food grease
Sprinkle talcum powder on the area, leave for five minutes, then brush off. Or cover with brown paper and press with a hot iron; the paper will soak up the grease.

MAKE-UP: SPRAY WITH HAIR SPRAY, BLOT AND REPEAT UNTIL THE STAIN IS REMOVED. WASH AS USUAL.

Grass
Treat with methylated spirit and rinse well with warm water. On nylon rub the stain with glycerine, leave for an hour and wash with soapy water.

Urine
Soak for an hour in a solution of one part hydrogen peroxide to six parts water plus a few drops of ammonia, then wash.

Wine
Red wine: pour white wine on the affected area, then wash in cold water and ammonia.

White wine: wash in cold water and ammonia.

44

CHAPTER 16

Shoes

Always put your right shoe on first and never walk around with one shoe missing or you will have bad luck for a year.

Never leave shoes on the table as this brings bad luck and will cause quarrelling in the house. Shoes or boots that are on the table should be placed on the floor before being worn. If you put your shoes on the bed, it will cause a death in the family.

It is bad luck if a beetle crawls out of your shoe, but if it crawls over it, this foretells death.

Never leave your shoes in the shape of a cross.

If the toes of your shoes wear out, it indicates that you are wasteful with money. If you have wear marks under the toes, you are a flirt; wear marks on the inside of the sole indicate a miser.

To drive away bad business, take a shoe from the oldest woman you can find and burn it in your place of work.

If you are a fisherman you should not go to sea if you see a flat footprint in the sand or if the person who is bringing your boots is carrying them over their shoulders, rather than under their arm.

If you are a coal miner, do not go down the pit if you wake up to find one of your boots has fallen over during the night.

A boxer should never wear new boots in a contest.

A young girl wishing to know who her true love will be should put one shoe across the other in the shape of a 'T' before she goes to bed and say: "I hope tonight my true love to see, so I put my shoes in the form of a "T"".

Cherry pickers should rub their shoes with cherry leaves to avoid choking on a cherry stone.

If your shoelace comes undone spontaneously, it is a sign that your true love is thinking of you. If they come undone while you are walking it means that your father loved you more than your mother. A broken shoelace brings bad luck.

During the winter, keep a red pepper in your shoes to keep your feet warm.

If you give a friend or lover a pair of shoes, they will walk out of your life. If you borrow a friend's shoes, an argument with them will soon follow.

Never accept the gift of an old pair of shoes or you will inherit the former owner's cares and misfortunes.

If you want to conceive a baby, try on the shoes of a woman who has just given birth.

If you hear a dog barking while you are lying in bed, you should reach under the bed and turn a shoe over, to ward off bad luck.

If a woman walks barefoot up to six weeks after giving birth, the baby will injure itself during a fall while it learns to walk.

Before playing cards, put your gaming shoes on before eating.

If a guest overstays their welcome, get rid of them by placing their shoe in the middle of a busy road and saying out loud that you wish them to leave.

\#

IF EVIL
SPIRITS OF
THE
DECEASED
ARE TROU-
BLING YOU,
BURN AN
OLD SHOE

If evil spirits of the deceased are troubling you, burn an old shoe with brimstone in a bucket and carry it to all four corners of the house.

Place a piece of jacinth in your shoe to guard against sickness or injury; it will also protect you against injury or sickness, and make people more cordial towards you.

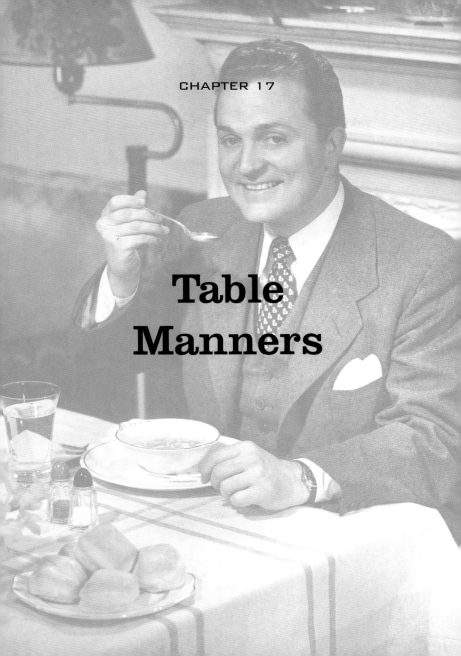

CHAPTER 17

Table Manners

As soon as you sit down, unfold your napkin and place it across your lap. Do not tuck it under your chin or leave it on the table. Only replace it on the table at the end of the meal. Do not use the napkin to mop your brow or face or blow your nose.

Do not season your food until you have tasted it. To do otherwise is an insult to the chef. Some would argue that to season your food at all is impolite.

Keep your elbows off the table and keep your hands on your lap or resting on the table.

When eating soup, scoop the spoon away from you and sip it from the side (do not place the whole spoon into your mouth), while avoiding slurping. When the soup level runs low, gently tilt the bowl away from you. Do not blow on your soup to cool it down. Do not allow the spoon to bang noisily on the bottom of the bowl.

Rolls and bread should be eaten by breaking off a small piece, buttering it (from a small supply which you have placed on the side of your plate) and eating. Repeat with the next piece and so on.
Do not under any circumstances leave the table during the meal unless you feel unwell. Make certain you visit the bathroom before the meal.

Do not do anything until your host has done it first. This includes sitting, drinking and eating. Never be the first to place your napkin back on the table at the end of the meal.

Use your utensils from the outside in. Once a piece of cutlery has been used it must not touch the table again, this includes leaning a handle on the tablecloth. This will reduce the risk of your dirtying the table linen.

#

DO NOT
SEASON
YOUR FOOD
UNTIL YOU
HAVE
TASTED IT.

When eating soup, scoop the spoon away from you and sip it from the side

Sit up straight in your chair and use your utensils to bring the food to your mouth. Do not bring your mouth to the food. You are the master, not the comestibles.

Avoid loud and boisterous talk and at all times be cheerful in conduct or conversation.

Never wear gloves at the table, unless for some reason your hands are unfit to be seen.

Do not chastise a waiter or servant for poor conduct; that is the privilege and responsibility of your host.

CHAPTER 18

Tea Time Etiquette

Check your tea invitation carefully. It may instruct you to bring your own special tea cup (as was the custom for Victorian ladies) or to wear a hat.

When pouring tea fill the cup three-quarters full and then ask "Would you like sugar? One lump or two?" Sugar lumps are preferable to the granulated variety as they are easier to handle and will dissolve nearly as easily. Offer milk or lemon (never cream, which curdles in tea).

Lemon should be sliced thinly so that each piece is light enough to float on top of the drink.

To hold your tea cup, pinch the handle between bent index finger and thumb. Do not loop your finger through the handle.

It is not necessary to extend your little finger; gently curve it into your palm (this obsolete ritual dates back to the time when all teacups were made in China without handles, so that the drinker was obliged to use thumb and index finger to hold the vessel and the pinkie for balance).

When stirring, do so noiselessly and swish the beverage back and forth rather than rotate the spoon in a single direction. Do not leave your spoon upright in the cup. Place it back on your saucer behind the cup on the right-hand side.

It may have been customary for Edwardian men to tip tea into their saucers to cool it down, but it is considered the height of bad manners today.

DO NOT PICK UP THE CUP LEAVING THE SAUCER ON THE TABLE.

If you are standing up and your cup and saucer are on the table, pick up both together. Do not pick up the cup leaving the saucer on the table. This is only

acceptable if you are sitting at a dining table. When
seated at a coffee table, always lift both items together.

When eating scones, place a small amount of cream
and jam on your plate then break off a small piece at a
time, add a small amount of jam and cream and place
in your mouth. Do not spread the entire scone or cut it
into two halves. No dipping.

On a three-tier cake stand, scones should be placed on
the top tier, savouries and sandwiches on the middle
and sweets on the bottom.

Always use sugar tongs, otherwise you risk infecting
the sugar bowl with germs when guests use their fingers. When not in use they should be hooked over the
handle of the sugar bowl.

High tea is served in the late afternoon or early
evening and takes the place of supper. Afternoon tea is
earlier and the food less substantial.

CHAPTER 19

Weather forecasting

Good weather

If you sneeze three times within a few seconds, the next day will be sunny.

The higher the clouds, the finer the weather. High clouds indicate that the air is dry and the pressure is high, which means good weather.

Rain

When the dew is on the grass, rain will never come to pass. Heavy dew on a summer night forms when skies are clear and the temperature has dropped.

Killing a spider will make it rain the next day.

When leaves show their backs, it will rain. Trees tend to grow leaves in a pattern according to the prevailing wind. Storm winds are naturally non-prevailing winds so when they occur, the leaves will be blown backwards and show their undersides.

Storms

If a bat lands on your head, it won't fly away until it hears thunder.

Swallows fly high when winds are light. So when they start flying low, a storm is brewing. The higher you go, the lower the air pressure. Migrating birds like to find their altitude limit and fly as high as they can. They are able to fly higher, due to the higher pressure in fair weather, than they can when a storm is coming.

Before a storm, cows will lie down or refuse to go out to pasture. When cows are lying down in a field it will remain fine; once they stand up rain is on its way.

IF YOU SNEEZE THREE TIMES WITHIN A FEW SECONDS, THE NEXT DAY WILL BE SUNNY.

It will be a bad winter
if there are lots of berries
on trees.

If a cat washes itself, expect good weather. But bad
weather may be expected if the cat licks its coat
against the grain, washes its face over its ears, or sits
with its tail to the fire.

Wind
If you throw away a dead mouse the wind will soon
blow from that direction.

Winter
It will be a bad winter . . .

If sheep gnash their teeth during roundup in the
autumn. If sheep gnash their teeth at another time, it
presages very bad weather.

If squirrels accumulate huge stores of nuts and have
thick bushy tails.

If there are lots of berries on trees.

If the first snow falls on unfrozen ground, expect a
mild winter.

CHAPTER 20

Basic Manners

Please . . . thank you . . . excuse me . . . you're welcome. Good manners are as important today as they were when your grandparents were born, because they help us to build and maintain better relationships. Let's wave goodbye to the nineties and look back to the nineteen nineties.

It is never acceptable to question someone about their health, finances or marital status, unless they brought up the topic themselves.

A man should always carry a woman's bags and never laugh at her mistakes.

Do not commit to something if your other commitments do not allow you to follow through. A polite refusal at the beginning is better than a job neglected or poorly performed later on.

Men should take the outside of the pavement when walking with or past a woman.

Do not rub the stomach of a pregnant woman. Respect her private space and body boundaries.

Mouth: keep it closed while chewing food and do not blow on hot food to cool it down.

After visiting a dual-sex lavatory, it is customary to leave the seat down.

Do not interrupt another person when they are speaking. When joining a group, do not change the topic of conversation.

Men should never smoke in front of a woman without first asking her permission.

Gloves: never appear in public without them. Do not smoke, eat or drink while wearing them. Remove them to play cards. Do not wear jewellery over them, except bracelets. Keep your gloves on in a receiving line or while dancing at a formal party and only remove them at a cocktail party after the drinks and hors d'oeuvres have passed. Always remove them at the dinner table.

Never shout, lose your temper or use foul language.

Men should never smoke in front of a woman without first asking her permission.

A man should tip his hat when walking with a friend they pass a woman only his friend knows; when a lady thanks him; when excusing himself to a female stranger; when someone shows courtesy to his female companion; when asking a woman or elderly man for directions.

A man should remove his hat when he is being introduced to someone, or saying goodbye; when greeting a lady on the street; while talking with a woman, older man or clergyman; at a funeral or when a funeral procession passes; when the National Anthem is being played.

CHAPTER 21

Baking Tips

cook book

Handle dough gently. If you are too rough the dough will become stronger and more difficult to handle.

To test the freshness of an egg, place it in a bowl of water. If it floats it is fresh. If it sinks it is older. Only use the freshest and finest ingredients when baking.

Remove bread, muffins and cakes from their metal tins as soon as they leave the oven. This prevents trapped steam from making the food soggy.

Cook cakes and cookies in the middle of the oven to allow heat to circulate evenly.

Toasting nuts such as almonds and pecans before using them in baking concentrates their flavour.

Whole wheat flour, wheat germ and wheat bran should be stored in the refrigerator to prevent the natural wheat oils from going rancid.

Bread stored at room temperature stays fresher longer than bread which is kept in the refrigerator.

To test if your yeast is still active, sprinkle a tablespoon of it in half a cup of lukewarm water in which has been dissolved a teaspoon of sugar. Stir and stand for ten minutes, by which time if the yeast is active it should have frothed up to fill the cup.

WHEN BAKING, ENSURE ALL YOUR INGREDI- ENTS ARE AT ROOM TEMPERA- TURE

When baking, ensure all your ingredients are at room temperature, so plan ahead and remove from the refrigerator in good time.

Always use large eggs when baking.

To ensure a clean cut slice of cheesecake, play your knife briefly above an open flame for a few seconds.

FOR A PRO-
FESSIONAL
SILKY
SHEEN TO
YOUR ICING,
BLOW DRY
WITH A
HAIRDRYER.

Wipe the blade and reheat between slices.

For a professional silky sheen to your icing, blow dry
with a hairdryer. This makes the surface melt slightly for a smooth and lustrous finish.

If your cakes sink or fall it is because of: overbeating,
underbaking, incorrect measurement of ingredients,
incorrect size of baking pan, opening the oven door
before the cake has set, incorrect oven temperature,
over- or undercreaming of butter and/or sugar.

Make your own self-raising flour by mixing
4 cups of flour with 2 teaspoons of salt and
2 tablespoons of baking powder. Store in an airtight
container,

To keep your brown sugar soft, store in an airtight
container with a slice of bread.

It is bad luck to bake bread on Halloween.

CHAPTER 22

Bygone Beauty

If you brush your hair more than 111 times a day, you or somebody very close to you will die.

Any pregnant woman who looks pretty must be having a boy because girls rob their mothers of beauty.

Washing your hair in rain water by the light of the full moon will make your hair soft.

Baking soda is an effective underarm deodorant. It is odourless, non toxic and works for hours.

To treat cellulite, rub coffee grounds into the affected area and drink up to three cups of green tea each day.

To keep your fingernails healthy and shiny, after cutting, soak them in vinegar to kill germs.

Place used tea bags on your eyelids to reduce puffiness. Keep a spoon in the freezer and apply to eyelids for a few minutes to reduce redness.

Dry brush your body with a natural bristle brush before taking a shower. It is a good way to stimulate the oil glands in your skin. Start at your feet and, brushing lightly in a circular motion, work up your body.

Rinse your hair once a week in apple-cider vinegar to remove toxins and shampoo and other hair product residues.

Before curling your eyelashes, heat the curler with a hair dryer for a few seconds. Test to make sure it is not too hot, then apply to your eyelashes. The heat will lock in the curl on extra long eyelashes.

Never sleep with a pillow. It will stop you getting wrinkles on your neck.

#

BAKING
SODA IS AN
EFFECTIVE
UNDERARM
DEODORANT.

Rinse your hair once a week in apple-cider vinegar to remove toxins and shampoo and other hair product residues.

Disinfect your telephone regularly. Germs on the ear piece can spread to your cheeks and give you spots. Also avoid touching your face during the day as you will transfer bacteria from your hands.

Exfoliate your whole body by mixing olive oil with a little sea salt or sugar. Rub gently using a circular movement and rinse off with a warm shower.

On the beach, make your hips and thighs look slim by scooping two little trenches under your thighs and make a hollow for your bottom. Cover your lower body with a towel and everyone will think you have perfect thighs and backside.

If you want to look five years younger get out of debt.

Cure your bunions with a poultice made from cow dung and fish oil. Apply warm and leave overnight.

Hair which is cut at the waning of the moon will stop growing.

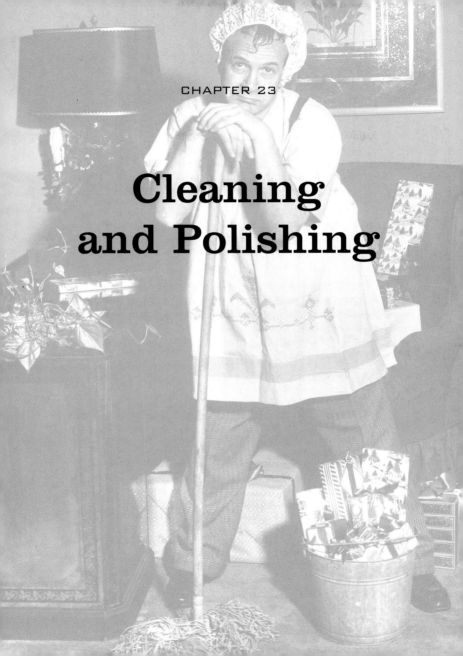

Cleaning
and Polishing

Drains

Pour one cup of salt and one cup of baking soda down the drain followed by 12 cups of boiling water. Allow to soak overnight and then flush with plenty of water.

Floors, Walls, Woodwork and Cupboards

Add 1/2 part of ammonia and one cup of washing soda to a one gallon demijohn or plastic jug. Add two cups of warm water and shake to dissolve the washing soda. Then top up the container with water. This can then be stored for future use. Use about ? cup per bucket of water for floors, or neat on tiles and enamel. Before use, check manufacturer's instructions for kitchen cupboards, kitchen work surfaces and other "modern" materials.

Homemade Furniture Polish

Add 1/2 teaspoon light olive oil to 1/2 cup white wine vinegar in a quart container. Top up with water.

Lime scale

Remove lime scale or waterline marks from a kettle or toilet bowl by adding two cups of white wine vinegar. Allow to soak overnight.

Windows

Use a 50/50 mixture of white wine vinegar and water. Use rolled up newspaper (not colour supplement) and soak in the solution. Squeeze to remove excess liquid. Rub the window with a circular motion. Dry with a fresh sheet of newspaper, making sure you remove all streaks (an indication that the window is still dirty).

Wood Restorer

Wear rubber gloves and keep the area well ventilated. Mix equal parts of boiled linseed oil, turpentine and white vinegar. Shake well. Rub into the grain with a soft, clean cloth. Wipe completely dry and wipe again with a fresh cloth.

Seven Time Savers

1. Set yourself a monthly schedule and stick to it. On a cleaning day set yourself a strict time limit, otherwise you will start daydreaming or get distracted and waste all day doing a job which should take a few hours.

2. Only clean what is dirty. For example, don't waste time cleaning an entire window if there are only a few marks in one corner.

3. Dust first, followed by vacuuming. Dust from top to bottom – this means starting at the top of a wall or shelf and working down.

4. Carry your cleaning materials with you in a supply apron or tool belt. Many people waste time searching for items, or cut corners by using the wrong tools or cleaners.

5. Rinse once. When you are scrubbing a surface, keep going until the dirt is removed. Then rinse. Repeated rinsing to check your progress wastes time.

6. Don't repeat yourself. Be methodical. Random acts of cleaning waste time. Start at one side of the house and work towards the other. Start at the door and work your way around each room in a clockwise direction. Then, if you are interrupted, it will be easier to resume where you left off.

7. Everything has its place. Clutter builds up because members of the household cannot agree where it should go. Everyone can actively maintain a clutter-free environment if they are in agreement.

#

DON'T REPEAT YOURSELF. BE METHODICAL.

CHAPTER 24

Fishing
Instruction

As soon as you count the number of fish you have caught, you will catch no more for the rest of the day.

Dolphins swimming with your ship are a sign of good luck. However, if a shark follows your boat then a death is imminent. Sharks have an ability to sense those who are close to death.

Always bait your hook with your right hand. Keep spitting on your bait. Don't let a woman step over your rods. Never use an upturned bucket as your seat.

Never bring a pig on board ship. Don't even say the word "pig" or "pork" for fear of being thrown over-board by your shipmates. The same goes for rabbits, eggs and bananas.

Before a fishing expedition, avoid meeting a fox, hare or unchurched woman.

Do not take pasties on board a fishing boat. They have corners – which is very unlucky.

If the herring season is good, always eat the herring from the tail forward to prolong the good fishing.

If you drop a knife while gutting fish on board a ship, if the tip points to land your next fishing trip will be inauspicious. If the knife points out to sea, next time you will catch all the fish your boat can carry.

Release your first catch of the day for good luck.

It is unlucky for a woman to be the first to ask you about your catch.

It is unlucky for a woman to comb her hair while her husband is at sea.

#

DO NOT TAKE PASTIES ON BOARD A FISHING BOAT.

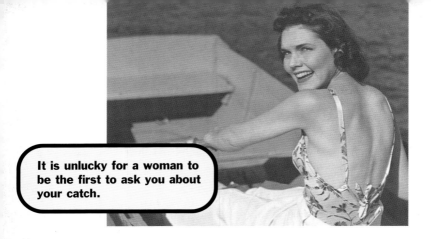

It is unlucky for a woman to be the first to ask you about your catch.

Never whistle on board.

If you go to your boat after dark, do not return to your house by the door unless someone lets you in. Climb through a window. This is because the witches leave butter on the door handle after dark. If you touch the witch butter your next day's catch will be beset with problems.

The feather of a wren which has been killed on New Year's Day can protect a fisherman against dying by shipwreck.

Lay the lungs of a cod on hot coals to predict the abundance of the forthcoming fishing season. If they roast gently the fishing will be favourable. If they explode, the season will be poor.

Do not rename your ship. Many vessels have been lost after a name change.

CHAPTER 25

Fruit and Vegetables

Prevent potatoes from budding by storing them with an apple.

Lemons are at their most lemony when they are at room temperature. Before squeezing, roll them under your palm on a table for maximum juiciness.

Ripen avocados and bananas by keeping them a brown paper bag with an apple.

Celery will stay crunchy for weeks when wrapped in aluminium and stored in the refrigerator.

If a stew or soup is too salty, drop a peeled potato into the pan to soak up some of the salt.

Add a few drops of lime or lemon juice to chopped avocados and apples to prevent them from turning brown.

Rub a cucumber with vinegar to remove the waxy film. Eat the skin – it's a good source of nutrition.

Use an egg slicer to save time when chopping mushrooms.

For tear free onions, store them in a refrigerator for an hour before cutting or run the onion under cold water or burn a candle as you slice it. Use a very sharp knife to prevent the onions from discolouring.

To remove the smell of onions from your hands, your fingers on the handle of a stainless steel spoon or sink, then run cold water over them.

Place a ripe tomato in a group of unripe ones. The ripe tomato will encourage the others to ripen.

#

USE AN
EGG SLICER
TO SAVE
TIME WHEN
CHOPPING
MUSH-
ROOMS.

A ripe, juicy apple eaten at bedtime every night will cure constipation

Adding two tablespoons of lemon juice or white vinegar to the saucepan stops cauliflower from going grey.

To remove the core from an iceberg lettuce, bash it down firmly on a table with the core side down, then twist and pull.

Restore limp celery by soaking in a bowl of ice water for an hour.

Keep fresh herbs in a plastic bag – blow into the bag before sealing. Fresh herbs like carbon dioxide.

Burn the scraps of your family's Christmas dinner around your fruit trees to ensure a good yield next year.

A ripe, juicy apple eaten at bedtime every night will cure constipation. An apple before bed is also good for sleeplessness and biliousness.

If you peel an orange without breaking the peel, you will get a new dress.

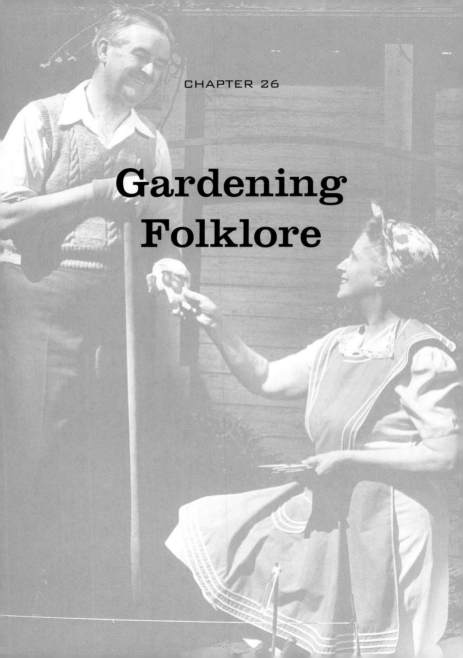

CHAPTER 26

Gardening Folklore

If you can't get someone to water your pot plants while you are away, place all of them in a children's inflatable paddling pool and fill with about three inches of water. That should keep them watered for a week.

Turn your pumpkins and marrows into monsters by feeding them with water using a round lamp wick. Make a hole in the stalk and insert one end of the wick and place the other end in a jar of water. The squashes should grow at twice their normal rate.

Dissolve 1oz of baking soda per gallon of water to control powdery mildew on climbing roses, cucumbers, aubergines and strawberries.

Plant on Good Friday to ensure a bountiful harvest. It is the one day of the year when the devil is powerless.

When sowing parsley, poor boiling water over the soil to deter the devil; then sow three rows: two for the devil and one for your crop.

Pour beer over your cabbages to increase the yield.

Cut several stems of willow and allow them to soak covered with an inch of warm water for a couple of days. Then dip your cuttings into this "willow tea" to assist them in rooting.

Throw rusty nails on the ground to boost the iron content in the soil. When planting a tree, throw a handful of rusty nails into the hole. They rust and release their iron slowly.

Catch slugs by leaving half a water melon on the ground with the flesh scooped out. The slugs climb inside and can't get out again.

#

POUR BEER OVER YOUR CABBAGES TO INCREASE THE YIELD.

After boiling beetroot, instead of throwing the purple water away, allow it to cool and then use it to water your plants.

BURY A
BOTTLE
HALFWAY
UNDER-
GROUND
AND LEAVE
A CHILD'S
WINDMILL
IN THE
BOTTLE.

Ward off deer by hanging a bar of soap from a tree, urinateing or spreading human hair on the ground.

Bury a bottle halfway underground and leave a child's windmill in the bottle. When the wind blows the spinning windmill will send vibrations through the soil to deter moles.

Cut potassium and potash-rich banana peel into small pieces and bury several inches deep around your rose bushes. Use no more than three skins per bush.

CHAPTER 27

Health

To cure a cough, shave your head and hang the hair on a bush so the birds may carry the hair and the cough back to their nests.

If you catch a falling leaf on the first day of autumn you will not catch a cold all winter.

A barefoot walk on the 1 May and before sunrise is a cure for sweating feet. Alternatively, wash your feet with your own urine.

A child can be protected from whooping cough by taking a ride on a bear's back.

A toothache can be cured by spitting into a frog's mouth and asking it to carry the pain away.

If you cross your eyes and the wind changes direction, they will stay that way.

To cure a cough, take a hair from your head, place it between two slices of well buttered bread and offer it to the dog with the words: "Eat well, you hound. May you be sick and I be sound."

Epilepsy and other fits can be avoided by wearing around the neck a silk bag containing the dried body of a frog.

If you ignore a wooden splinter and fail to remove it from your body, it will grow into a tree.

Treat chilblains by carrying horse's teeth or by pricking the area with a holly leaf. Alternatively, keep a piece of Christmas cake or Yule log under the bed.

To have good health throughout the next year, eat an apple on Christmas Eve.

#

TO CURE
A COUGH,
SHAVE
YOUR HEAD
AND HANG
THE HAIR
ON A
BUSH...

Ease a sore throat by sleeping with a smelly sock around your neck.

Drink a glass of milk and a biscuit before bedtime to help you to sleep. Otherwise do not eat within three hours of going to bed.

Cracking your knuckles causes arthritis; kicking a cat gives you rheumatism; crossing your legs causes varicose veins.

When you feel sickness approaching, place a clove of peeled garlic in your mouth and leave it there for as long as you can. Then chop it up, leave it for 20 minutes and eat.

Shivering for no reason is a sign that someone has just walked over the place where you will be buried when you die.

Drink a glass of hot milk with a teaspoon of clarified butter at bedtime to ease constipation.

Cure bleeding gums by drinking a cup of water with the juice of half a lemon and one teaspoonful of honey every morning; massage your gums with a little coconut oil.

For aching muscles apply a homemade balm to the affected area. It consists of one tablespoon of horseradish sauce in 1/2 cup of olive oil.

DRINK A GLASS OF MILK AND A BISCUIT BEFORE BEDTIME TO HELP YOU TO SLEEP.

CHAPTER 28

How to Behave at a Funeral

There's no single "right" way to act at a funeral, but there are plenty of ways to act "wrong". People often do and say inappropriate things when they feel awkward, and a funeral is no exception.

Dress in dark grey, navy or black clothes. It is better to dress too formal than appear too casual. For a Jewish funeral bring a yarmulke (skull cap, kippah).

Turn off your mobile phone and arrive early.

Pay your respects to the bereaved if you feel able. The following are acceptable: "I'm so sorry"; "If there is anything we/I can do . . ."; "S/he will be greatly missed"; "We will always remember him/her".

Do not say: "At least his/her suffering is over"; "At least it was quick"; "Everything happens for a reason . . ."

Remember that your presence at the funeral is noted and appreciated, even if you feel unable to offer words of condolence. Do not expect to be able to say anything that makes the bereaved feel better.

It is acceptable to cry, even if you feel you didn't know the deceased very well. Try not to draw attention but conduct yourself in a sincere and authentic manner.

Find out beforehand whether it is acceptable to send flowers. Some people prefer donations to be made to charity; some religions forbid them.

You may be expected to bring food for the bereaved family.

If you are asked to give a eulogy, it is your duty to accept the honour. It should express positively how you feel about the deceased and should be dignified, heartfelt and personal.

Do not take photographs.

Funeral Lore
Nothing new should be worn to a funeral, especially shoes.

Pregnant women should not attend funerals.

It is bad luck to meet a funeral procession head on.

If a funeral car passes you should hide your thumb.

Seeing a white chicken on your way to a funeral brings bad luck.

If rain falls on a funeral procession someone related to the deceased will die in the near future.

#

IT IS BETTER TO DRESS TOO FORMAL THAN APPEAR TOO CASUAL.

CHAPTER 29

How to Behave at the Opera

Dress

Though some purists lament the fact that nobody wears waistcoats and formal attire to the opera any more, in fact you can wear whatever you choose, although many people still see it as a good excuse to dress up. If in doubt, dress up rather than down. Some opera goers wear black tie and evening dresses, while others feel comfortable in jeans.

Timing

Always arrive early. If you are late you may not be allowed into the auditorium until after the overture, and may even have to wait as long as the end of the first act. There are no ticket refunds for latecomers,

even those who have had to wait for 40 minutes in
the foyer.

Seating
When you are required to pass others to reach your
seat, do not shuffle down the row with your backside
in their faces. Turn around, smile and face them as
you pass, rather than give them a plum view of your
rear end.

Applause
After the orchestra have tuned their instruments,
acknowledge the entry of the conductor with
applause. It is appropriate to applaud after the overture and at the end of an act (and sometimes a scene).
It is also common for audiences to applaud after an
aria. Don't just applaud an aria because you recog-
nise the tune. Applause should be an acknowledge-
ment of a good performance. Don't clap after every
aria, since this can lead to numerous interruptions
which break the dramatic flow. If you are unsure, follow the lead of the rest of the audience, but remember
that operas are live performances and the performers
enjoy well-placed appreciation.

Noise
Switch off your mobile phone and digital watch
alarm. If you must cough, try to do it during the
loud bits. Don't sing along, hum the tune, or sway in
time with the music. Nobody likes a noise maker or
show off. Leave food at home and do not talk during
the overture – it is an important part of the performance. Do not read your programme during the performance.

Bravo, Brava, Bravi
At the curtain call, feel free to shout out "Bravo!" for
a male performer, "Brava!" for a female and "Bravi!"
for a group of performers.

#

APPLAUSE
SHOULD BE
AN
ACKNOW-
LEDGEMENT
OF A GOOD
PERFORM-
ANCE.

CHAPTER 30

How to Make Jam

1. Put six cups each of washed fruit and sugar into a large saucepan with a little water or the juice of one lemon.

2. Simmer gently for up to an hour while stirring in a large figure of eight and mashing the fruit with a wooden spoon, making sure that all the sugar is dissolved. Scrape the bottom of the pan regularly to stop the mixture from sticking.

3. When the sugar has dissolved, turn up the heat and cook rapidly at a rolling boil (one that cannot be stirred down), stirring slowly to prevent burning. Do not stir quickly or beat the mixture at this point.

4. To test whether the jam is ready for jarring, do the cooling test: place a tablespoonful of the jam on ice-cold plate and let it cool for one minute. If the cool jam wrinkles when you scrape it off, the mixture is ready.

5. Wash and boil the jam jars to sterilise them (use the sterilise function on your dishwasher). Pour the jam into the jars while they are still hot. This prevents the jars from cracking. Fill within a 1/2 an inch of the top and then seal with paraffin wax.

The consistency of the jam depends on the amount of pectin in the fruit. Apples, quinces, red currants, plums, gooseberries and cranberries contain a lot of pectin. Jams made from low pectin fruits such as strawberries, blueberries, peaches, apricots, cherries, blackberries and raspberries may require extra pectin to help them to set.

THE CON-
SISTENCY
OF THE JAM
DEPENDS
ON THE
AMOUNT OF
PECTIN IN
THE FRUIT.

Always use fresh ripe fruit for a full flavour. If fruit is overripe its pectin content is much lower and the jam may not set.

Remove the hulls from strawberries; with other berries just remove stems, leaves and stones. Cook the stones in a muslin bag to flavour the jam.

Finely chop fruit but do not puree as this will generate too much liquid and make the jam too runny.

Make jam in small batches. If you try to make too much in one go the jam will not set.

Add a knob of butter to the jam to reduce the amount of froth on top.

Rubbing the jam pan with butter before use makes it easier to clean afterwards.

CHAPTER 31

How to Write a Love Letter

Two fates await the written expression of love for the object of your undying affection. Your words will either be kept or burned. But will they be worth reading? Here are some words on the lost art of love letter composition.

Write from the heart and with the utmost regard for perfection. It matters not whether you are an accomplished writer. If you are sincere, honest and caring, your words will find a natural rhythm and music.

Acquire high quality parchment and handwrite in ink. If your handwriting is worse than a physician's, employ a skilled calligrapher to transcribe your words. The visual impression will create a romantic disposition in your quarry before they even begin to read.

Be attentive to your spelling and punctuation. Love may be blind, but it notices those unschooled in the rudiments of good grammar.

Ladies should be careful to maintain their dignity when writing. A love letter should not be written lightly, for the consequences of idly toying with the affections of another can be grave.

Avoid purple prose – simple writing is easier to read and more sincere than obscure vocabulary.

Place a photograph of your loved one in front of you. Take your time and begin slowly.

Listen to some romantic music to give you inspiration while you compose: Frederic Chopin, Ludwig

LISTEN TO SOME ROMANTIC MUSIC TO GIVE YOU INSPIRATION WHILE YOU COMPOSE

Beethoven, Georges Bizet, Claude Debussy, Gustav Mahler, Felix Mendelssohn, Sergei Rachmaninov, Jean Sibelius, Peter Ilyich Tchaikovsky or Richard Wagner.

A love letter need not be earnest – the tone can be playful, flirtatious or witty. Whatever tone you choose must feel comfortable and express your voice. Write as you speak and think. Do not attempt to be Andrew Marvell if John Keats is more your style.

POINT OUT TWELVE UNIQUE QUALITIES ABOUT YOUR BELOVED WHICH YOU LOVE.

Be specific. Point out 12 unique qualities about your beloved which you love. Present each one as you would a red rose – with simplicity. Carefully-chosen words, like beautiful flowers, need no other adornments but themselves.

Write only about the two of you and nothing else.

End the letter by looking to the future. You want this relationship to last forever, growing year by year. Let them know your thoughts and hopes for your life together.

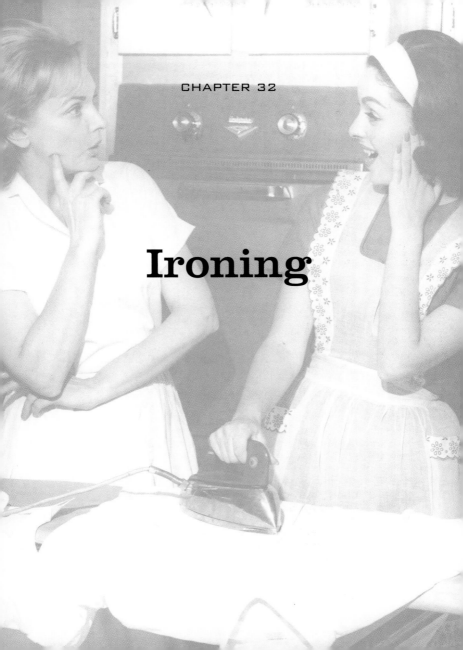

Ironing

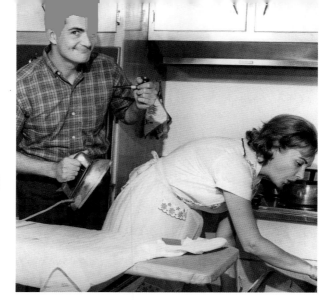

DON'T
WEAR
SOMETHING
IMMEDIATE-
LY AFTER IT
HAS BEEN
IRONED

Add one tablespoon of ammonia to each cup of water in your iron. This softens the water and makes ironing smoother.

To clean the base of your iron, unplug and rub with a cloth dipped in methylated spirit or vinegar.

To stop your iron from sticking to delicate fabrics, sprinkle a rag with talcum powder and use it occasionally to dust the bottom of the iron.

Rubbing the inside of a trouser crease with a piece of wet soap helps it to stay in place while you iron.

Don't wear something immediately after it has been ironed, as it will crease easily. Allow it to cool down for at least half an hour.

Keep linen laundry in a plastic bag in the refrigerator or freezer for several hours before ironing. This makes it easier to iron and prevents mildew.

When using starch, first spray the underside of the garment; then roll the clothing into a ball. This allows the fabric to absorb the moisture before ironing.

Do not use circular strokes, as they stretch the fabric. For tough wrinkles, iron lengthwise and use a burst of steam.

Never iron dirty or stained clothing as it could permanently set stains into the fabric.

Rinsing clothes in cool water (or using the permanent press cycle on your washing machine) is key to preventing wrinkles and reduces time spent ironing.

How to iron a shirt
1. Set your iron the temperature indicated on the shirt label.
2. Iron while your shirt is a little damp.
3. Undo all the buttons.
4. Iron to the back of the collar, working from the points to the centre; turn over and repeat on the front.
5. Place the shirt shoulders face down over the board and iron the shoulders (called the "yoke").
6. Next iron the sleeves, first with the seams touching, then again with the seams parallel. Do not create a crease.
7. Pull the cuffs tight to stretch out the wrinkles while you iron – inside first then the outside.
8. Press the front buttoned panel, the back, then the button-hole front panel, keeping the material taut to smooth creases.
9. Allow to cool completely on a hanger before wearing. Do up the top three buttons to retain the shape.

CHAPTER 33

Kitchen Witchery

Always break the shell of an egg completely; otherwise a witch may use it as a boat.

Throw away unwanted bread and you will go hungry.

Soak up excess fat in your soup by floating a large lettuce leaf on the surface.

When a loved one travels away on a long journey, hang a sprig of sage in the kitchen. As long as it remains healthy, they will have pleasant travels.

To keep cottage cheese fresh for longer, turn the container upside down in the refrigerator.

Add two teaspoons of lemon to a broth-based soup for a savoury treat.

Keep a pot of basil growing in your kitchen to ward off evil spirits.

Do not wash your frying pan. Instead, scour it with salt and oil.

To discourage mould from forming on cheese, leave a few cubes of sugar wrapped up with it.

Keep an onion on the kitchen windowsill to absorb ill will. When it becomes rotten, throw it away and replace with a fresh one.

If a coffee pot keeps boiling over or if you keep spilling water on the tablecloth, a storm is brewing.

#

If your apron comes untied and falls off while you are working in the kitchen, someone (usually your sweetheart) is thinking about you.

DO NOT WASH YOUR FRYING PAN.

Salt is precious. When you spill salt, throw a little over your left shoulder to blind the devil and stop him from seeing your folly and taking your soul.

If someone brings a hoe into your house and does not go directly to the kitchen and then leave by the front door again, there will soon be a death in the family.

A quartz crystal placed on or near the stove when cooking improves the taste of the food.

The most auspicious time to plant an herb garden is when the moon is in Cancer, Scorpio, Libra or Pisces.

Keep an aloe vera plant in your kitchen and squeeze the juice from a mature fleshy stalk onto minor stove burns to soothe and heal them.

If you want to have success with an untried recipe, copy it out in red ink and place it on the kitchen table. Then place a red candle in a holder on top of the recipe and allow it to burn down completely before attempting the recipe.

Leave a pinch of sifted flour in a dark corner of your kitchen to attract wealth.

So long as you keep a small jar of alfalfa in your larder, your family will never go hungry.

CHAPTER 34

Recycling

YOU CAN HELP
THROW IT HERE

Where possible buy in bulk. It saves money and it reduces packaging waste.

Write "Unsolicited mail: return to sender" on your junk mail and send it back. Disposing of the paper becomes their responsibility.

Discover your local library and always borrow a book or newspaper rather than buy one.

Don't use cling film and aluminium foil to store food. Use washable containers with lids such as ice cream, margarine or paté.

Save all your candle stumps, melt them down, tie a wick over a lolly stick and rest the stick on top of a jam jar so the wick is dead centre. Then pour in the molten wax to make another candle.

Rather than leave old paint pots in the garage, give them away to theatre groups or art projects.

Turn an old worn out bath mat into a floor cloth. Fold it and fit it into the mop handle. It can even be washed after use.

Make a cat or dog collar from an old belt.

Ironing board covers usually wear out in one or two places. Cut up and use the other areas to make an oven mitt or pan holder.

Make new napkins from worn tablecloths.

Re-use the zippers from old clothes. Shorten a zipper by sewing a zigzag stick across the bottom end.

Remove the bottom from a yoghurt pot and place it round delicate shoots and plants to protect them from the wind and cold during the spring.

Discover your local library and always borrow a book or newspaper rather than buy one.

Collect all your old pieces of soap and place them in the leg of an old pair of nylons to make a gardening scrubber to clean your hands.

Use a refillable ink pen rather than a disposable biro. Your handwriting will be better and your waste minimal.

Take old magazines to your dentist or doctor's surgery.

CHAPTER 35

Parenting Wisdom

Do not tickle your baby's feet; it will make him develop a stutter when he learns to talk.

It is unlucky to cut or wash a baby's hair until it is over a year old.

After you have cut your child's hair, burn the clippings, so that nobody can do them harm by getting hold of the hair and using it for witchcraft.

If you wash a child's hands before his first birthday he will grow up poor.

Do not cut nails; a child's nails should be bitten, lest he becomes a thief. If you must cut nails, allow the clippings to fall on the Bible.

When a child loses its milk teeth they should be burned otherwise the new teeth will grow crooked.

To soothe your baby during teething, it should wear a coral necklace. They will change colour depending on the baby's health.

Babies with blue veins on their noses will not see their 21st birthday.

Do not lay a newborn child on its left side or it will grow up to be clumsy.

Nurse your baby while sitting on the boundary stone at a fork in the road to prevent toothaches.

Do not hamper your children by making their lives too easy.

Keep cats away from infants; they suck the breath of the child.

#

DO NOT LAY A NEW-BORN CHILD ON ITS LEFT SIDE OR IT WILL GROW UP TO BE CLUMSY.

Place a red ribbon on the cot of a child who has been ill to prevent the ague from returning.

The mother should hide the baby's first shorn lock so that fate will smile down on her child during her life.

If a child captures a ladybird and then lets it go again, if it flies straight up or behind them, the person they will grow up to marry will the next day stand at the place where the ladybird was released.

If a child has a birthmark it marks the spot where a mortal wound was inflicted in a previous reincarnation.

White spots on a child's fingernails are a tell-tale sign that they have lied.

If a mother keeps her child's cord stump, it will grow up to be intelligent. Better still, she should sew it into a little red triangular pouch and fix it to the baby's clothes to keep her from harm.

Children with two crowns will grow up to be success-ful with money and will never drown or emigrate.

Relaxation and sleep

MAKE THE
FOOT OF
THE BED
BEFORE THE
HEAD, OR
ELSE MY
DEAR,
YOU'LL
NEVER WED.

Dreams at night are a devil's delight, Dreams in the morning, heed the angels' warning.

Before sleeping or to relieve stress, grip your earlobes gently between forefingers and thumbs and move them in circles in opposite directions while counting to ten.

Rub a few drops of pure lavender oil into your temples to ease a headache and drip them onto your pillow to help you sleep.

Never turn your mattress on a Sunday, or you'll have nightmares.

After a wedding, a young woman who wishes to dream of her future spouse should sleep with a piece of wedding cake under her pillow. At other times, rose petals under the pillow or rubbing herself with marjoram have the same effect.

When it comes to choosing a mattress, hard is better.

Getting out of bed on the "wrong side" brings bad luck. It means that you climbed in on one side and left from the other.

Sleeping with a sunflower under your bed will allow you to know the truth in any matter.

A teaspoon of honey before bed prevents bedwetting. Children who play with fire will wet the bed regardless.

Make the foot of the bed before the head, or else my dear, you'll never wed.

If you reveal your dream or nightmare to someone before you have eaten breakfast, it will come true.

When it comes to choosing a mattress, hard is better.

If you have the same dream three times in a row, it will come true.

If a spider crawls across your bed, expect a visit from a stranger.

If you sneeze before getting out of bed, you will have bad luck all day.

To cure a person of snoring, place an axe under their pillow, sew a tennis ball into the back of their night-shirt to stop them lying on their back, or bury a tuft of their hair under a willow tree by moonlight.

To avoid bed sores, sleep with a couple of buckets of spring water beneath your bed.

If a young woman falls asleep at work, she will marry a widower. To make her feel more alert, she should remove her socks and put them underneath her desk.

CHAPTER 37

Replying to an Invitation

Whatever the event – wedding, dinner party or fund raiser – an invitation obliges you to take careful consideration of those who have invited you, and so you must familiarise yourself with the appropriate response.

When an invitation contains the letters RSVP, it means "Répondez, s'il vous plaît," or, "Please reply." Do so without delay – you should reply within two days of receiving an invitation because the organiser requires a definite head count.

Suit the formality of the reply to the manner of the invitation. If there is a response card, fill it in by the date shown and return in an envelope. Reply to a formal invitation with no accompanying response card with a handwritten letter worded thus:

Mr/Mrs/Ms [your full name
(or names if two people are invited)],
accept with pleasure/regret that they are
unable to accept/regret that a previous engagement
prevents their accepting
[host or hosts' full name/s as printed
on the invitation]
kind invitation for
[day of the week and date as printed
on the invitation]

If a phone number is included on the RSVP invitation, you may telephone your response. Make sure you speak to the host in person, as an answering machine message does not always reach its intended listener.

EVEN IF
THERE IS
NO RSVP,
IT IS STILL
POLITE TO
LET YOUR
HOSTS
KNOW YOUR
INTEN-
TIONS.

If the invitation states "regrets only" then you need only reply if you are unable to attend.

Even if there is no RSVP, it is still polite to let your hosts know your intentions.

Once you have accepted an invitation, illness or bereavement are the only acceptable excuses for breaking your commitment to attend the function. You may change a "no" to a "yes", but only if it does not disrupt the arrangements of the hosts.

Do not bring uninvited guests and do not presume to ask if you may. An invitation is extended only to those written on it. Do not assume that an invitation to a married couple also includes the children, if their names or the words "and family" are absent from the invitation.

When invited to the church only at a wedding, a reply is usually not required.

Excuse yourself from invitations where the feelings, habits and dispositions of the hosts are reverse of your own, for there can be no pleasure in familiar intercourse where there is no congeniality.

CHAPTER 38

Sewing

If you sew on Sunday, the devil will thread the needle and when you reach heaven you will have to unpick the stitches with your nose.

It is unlucky to drop a pair of scissors. However, you can ward off this bad luck by putting your foot on the scissors before you pick them up.

Scissors should not be left open so that the blades form the shape of a cross. If the scissors are left in this way it brings bad luck for the person who wears the garment you are making.

Avoid sewing a button or repairing a garment while you are wearing it otherwise you will develop a serious illness that will last for a month and destroy your chances of making a good living. If you have to patch a tear while wearing a garment, hold a pin in your mouth to protect against bad luck.

After a quilt has been completed, the quilter should sleep under it for one night before passing it on to the loved one for whom it was made.

It is unlucky to pass a pin and not pick it up. See a pin and let it lie, sure to rue it by and by.

Never lend a pin to a friend, lest it should prick your friendship. If you present a friend with a new packet of needles, remove one of them and prick them with it to protect them from ill fortune.

Throwing a bent or crooked pin into a wishing well brings good luck.

Dropping a needle brings good luck. If it sticks upright in the floor, expect company.

#

THROWING A BENT OR CROOKED PIN INTO A WISHING WELL BRINGS GOOD LUCK.

When you break a needle it is a sign that one of your friendships is in trouble.

Rubbing starch on your thread will make it pass more easily through the eye of the needle.

Clear nail polish is the best remedy for a run in a pair of nylons.

Store your pantyhose in the freezer to make it last longer. Apply hairspray to the toes to prevent wear.

To free up a stiff zipper, rub with starch or a candle.

To see if someone is lying, suspend a needle by a thread above a copy of the Bible and say the person's name three times. If the needle is steady, they are telling the truth; if the needle moves around they are lying.

CHAPTER 39

Ten Traditional Hangover Cures

"Man, being reasonable, must get drunk," observed Lord Byron. Unfortunately the next morning a hangover can attack you on all fronts.

Alcohol dilates the blood vessels, which gives you poor circulation and a resultant headache. It encourages your kidneys to excrete urine, so you feel dehydrated, plus you lose important body salts called electrolytes. Alcohol irritates the stomach lining, to give you an upset tummy, and you'll also have low blood sugar and fatigue. Here are ten traditional ways to beat the hangover blues:

Prairie Oyster
Crack a raw egg in a highball glass. Add a shot of brandy (optional) and two dashes each of Worcestershire sauce and Tabasco sauce. Swallow in one without chewing, allowing the unbroken yolk to slide down your throat. Alternatively drop an egg yolk into a glass of orange juice and down in one for a Bull's Eye. (Please note: raw eggs may contain salmonella – eat at your own peril.)

Ye Fulle English breakfast
Complete with two fried eggs, bacon, sausages, black pudding, mushrooms, fried bread, baked beans, lamb kidney and tomato, washed down with plenty of water or fruit juice, or a little hair of the dog: half a pint of London Pride. ("I pray thee let me and my fellow have a haire of the dog that bit us last night," wrote John Heywood in 1546.)

Yoghurt Smoothy
Beat a pint of cold water gradually into a pint of live plain yoghurt. Add two tablespoons of chopped mint and salt to taste, then liquidize until smooth. There

should be enough for you and three of your hung-over friends.

BRAT
Eat BRAT (bananas, rice, apple sauce and toast/crackers) because they are mild foods that won't upset your stomach.

Bloody Mary
Over crushed ice, mix a shot of vodka with three drops of Tabasco sauce, 4oz of tomato juice, freshly ground black pepper, the juice of one lemon, a pinch of salt and a teaspoon of Worcestershire sauce. Strain and serve with ice in a tall glass. Drink with a wet cold towel wrapped around your forehead, or better still, while taking a cold shower.

Lemon Rub
Rub half a lemon under each armpit, anticlockwise.

Vinegar Coleslaw
Finely grate half a white cabbage with two large carrots and half an onion. Stir in two tablespoons of apple cider vinegar and some salad cream or mayonnaise for a creamy texture. Crunch away.

Café et du sel
A timeless French remedy consisting of strong black coffee with salt. Why not enjoy with a French omelette and a pain au chocolate.

Go Back to Bed
Nobody can extol the virtues of sleep better than Lady Macbeth, an expert in the morning after feeling:

Go Back to Bed

"Sleep that knits up the ravelled sleave of care,
The death of each day's life, sore labour's bath,
Balm of hurt minds, great Nature's second course,
Chief nourisher in life's feast."

Chew Charcoal
Eating a little charcoal helps to clear out the toxins in
your body. It is used in water filters for its cleansing
properties; you can buy charcoal tablets at the phar-
macist.

CHAPTER 40

Twenty Rules to Live By

1. Do not walk into a snake pit with your eyes open.
2. One simple maxim is worth more than two good friends.
3. When rain falls on your roof, remember that it falls on others' as well.
4. God gave us nuts, but we must crack them ourselves.
5. Learn manners by observing those who have none.
6. You cannot see the whole sky through a stick of bamboo.
7. Do not choose your bride at a dance; watch her in the field at harvest time.
8. Those who wish to sing can always find a song.
9. Do not throw away your old bucket until you are certain that your new one holds water.
10. Do not let your feet run faster than your shoes.
11. If one man's beard is on fire, another man may warm his hands by it.
12. You need big bait to catch a big fish.
13. The mediocre climb molehills and do not get out of breath.
14. If you destroy a bridge, first make sure you can swim.
15. If you are looking for a fly in your food, it is a sign that you are full.
16. Every fish that escapes appears greater than it is.
17. If you are in a hurry, take a roundabout route.
18. If you are afraid to put your foot down, don't be surprised when other people step on your toes.
19. Birds may be blessed with the gift of flight, but remember that they also eat worms.
20. Stay in bed until noon only after you have gained a reputation for rising early.

CHAPTER 41

Washing

Washing clothes on Holy Thursday will cause a death in the family by washing a relative away.

A traditional alternative to bleach in your wash: use half a cup of lemon juice or 1/4 cup of white vinegar.

When whites become faded, freshen them up by soaking them for half an hour in a bowl of boiling water into which you have placed half a lemon sliced thinly. Then wash as usual. Dissolve a tablespoon of borax in a pint of hot water and add it to the rinse cycle.

Moisten an old cloth with liquid softener and place in your tumble drier as an alternative to a costly and wasteful sheet fabric softener.

To prevent pilling, turn delicate garments inside out before washing.

To make an itchy woollen sweater more comfortable, wash in warm water with two tablespoons of glycerine.

To restore the brightness of white woollens, after washing place them in the freezer for half an hour. The cold has a mild bleaching effect. Thaw and dry normally.

#

To soften jeans add 1/4 cup of salt to your wash.

Tie delicate items inside a pillowcase before placing in the washing machine.

Adding ? cup of white vinegar to the rinse cycle has the same effect as using expensive commercial fabric softeners, with the added benefit of brightening colours and fighting mould and fungus. Once dry, your clothes will not smell of vinegar!

TIE DELI-
CATE ITEMS
INSIDE A
PILLOWCASE
BEFORE
PLACING IN
THE
WASHING
MACHINE.

\#

WHITEN
YELLOWED
LACE BY
SOAKING IT
IN SOUR
MILK.

Place a wet towel or a ball of aluminium foil in the tumble drier with delicates to prevent them from overdrying and developing static.

Drying garments in the tumble dryer makes them wear out much quicker because it rubs the fibres together. Dry your washing in the breeze for longer wearing clothes.

Hanging coloured garments in direct sunlight all day will make them fade. As soon as they are dry, bring them inside.

Whiten yellowed lace by soaking it in sour milk.

Make your own laundry detergent: flake a bar of soap into a saucepan of hot water and heat until it dissolves. Then add the soap solution to three gallons of hot water, stir well and then stir in a cup of washing soda. Let it cool. Use one cupful in each load of washing to make considerable savings.

CHAPTER 42

Cats and Dogs

Cats

A cat sneezing is a good omen for everyone who hears it.

When you see a one-eyed cat, spit on your thumb, stamp it in the palm of your hand, and make a wish. The wish will come true.

If a cat washes behind its ears, it will rain.

When a cat is sleeping with all four paws tucked under, cold weather is on its way.

It is bad luck to cross a stream carrying a cat.

Two cats seen fighting near a dying person, or on the grave shortly after a funeral, are the devil and an angel fighting for possession of the soul.

When moving house, put the cat through the window of the new home instead of the door, so that it will not be tempted to stray.

Cats spread gossip, so do not allow the cat in the room when you are discussing family affairs.

IF A CAT WASHES BEHIND ITS EARS, IT WILL RAIN.

Cat dreams: Dream of a tortoiseshell = lucky in love; ginger cat = lucky in money and business; black-and-white cat = luck with children; tabby = domestic luck; multicoloured cat = luck making friends.

Dogs

A newborn baby licked by a dog will always be a fast healer.

When a dog eats grass, it is going to rain.

A strange dog coming to the house presages a new friendship.

It is lucky to meet a spotted or black-and-white dog on the way to a business meeting.

Seeing three white dogs together brings good luck.

If you want to see a spirit, put wax from a dog's eye into yours.

If a dog runs between a woman's legs, her husband will beat her.

Young single women should take notice of where the dogs bark on Saint Andrew's Eve; her groom will come from this direction.

SEEING THREE WHITE DOGS TOGETHER BRINGS GOOD LUCK.

CHAPTER 43

Do It Yourself

Before papering or painting a room, paint over any grease spots on the wall with a thin coat of white shellac to prevent the grease from penetrating the new wallpaper or paint.

Lubricate door hinges with petroleum jelly, as oil may run and dirty the paintwork.

Mix black pepper with your window putty to discourage birds from pecking it away.

When you have finished wallpapering a room, write on the top of the room door how many rolls you used; the next person who has to do the job won't have to measure up.

Leave a bucket of water or a plate of sliced apples in a freshly-painted room to remove the smell of paint.

If you can't be bothered to wash your brushes overnight, place them in a plastic bag and store them in the freezer.

When painting outside, prevent splash marks by spreading sand on the ground below the area to be painted.

Soften old hard paint brushes by soaking them in hot vinegar and then combing them with an old fork.

For stability, a ladder should be one foot out for every four feet in height.

To loosen rusty screws, soak them overnight in lemon juice.

Brighten up grubby sash cord for windows and bathroom light pulls by painting with white canvas shoe cleaner.

#

MIX BLACK PEPPER WITH YOUR WINDOW PUTTY TO DISCOURAGE BIRDS FROM PECKING IT AWAY.

Smear a new screw with grease or soap and it will be easier to remove. For a tighter fit, paint on a little nail varnish and screw it while wet.

Mark a drill bit with masking tape at the desired depth to prevent you from drilling too deeply into a surface.

When drilling glazed surfaces, cover the spot with clear adhesive tape to prevent the drill bit from slipping.

Do not allow drill bits to overheat or they will become damaged.

When attaching a radiator to an outside wall, paste tin foil to the wall behind it to reflect back the heat.

Always cut away from your hands, not towards them.

Use a bent straw to blow dust from freshly drilled holes.

When replacing a tap, always put the plug in the sink before you begin, then you won't lose any small parts down the drain.

#

ALWAYS
CUT AWAY
FROM YOUR
HANDS,
NOT
TOWARDS
THEM.

CHAPTER 44

Everyday Hygiene

# #

AVOID
STAYING IN
THE BATH-
ROOM TOO
LONG AS
THIS WILL
MAKE YOUR
FACE
APPEAR
OLD.

Wash behind your ears each day or potatoes will grow there.

Comb mayonnaise, olive oil, tea three oil and petroleum jelly into your hair to get rid of head lice (also known as cooties or nits).

If you dream of washing your face, it expresses your need to atone for some indiscretion.

If one goes to bed without washing one's feet, they will lie in the fires of Hell.

Sitting on cushions causes boils on your buttocks.

Drinking water from the lavatory makes a man a liar.

Do not take a bath or shower during the afternoon as this makes you age faster.

If the milkmaid or milkman doesn't wash his hands after attending to each cow the yield of the herd will diminish.

Avoid staying in the bathroom too long as this will make your face appear old.

On the day of an exam or important test, do not wash your hair as it will clean your memories away and everything you have learned will be washed out of your head.

If two people wash their hands together in the same basin they are courting disaster.

If you wash in water which has been previously used by someone else, you will soon quarrel with them. To break the spell, you must clasp your hands together over the water after washing them.

If you dream of washing your face, it expresses your need to atone for some indiscretion.

He who laughs at his father or mother-in-law will develop a stye.

Washing your hands in moonlight will cure you of warts.

If you are on a winning streak, do not change your socks until after you lose.

You should wash your face after escorting a coffin to its grave in order to avoid being followed by the ghost of the deceased.

Each time you wash your body, you wash away some of your life essence.

CHAPTER 45

Hedgerow Foraging

Gleaning tasty goodies from the hedgerows is very rewarding. It gives you fresh air and exercise and the reward of some delicious food at the end of your excursion.

Pack enough supplies for a day trip. You don't know how long you will be tempted to stay picking. Pack disposable wipes and plenty of drinking water and lots of empty containers – there is nothing worse than running out of room when the hedgerows are abundant. When picking, leave the lids off so moisture doesn't build up.

Wear old and comfortable shoes and clothes that you don't mind snagging on a bush or staining with fruit juice. Take a wide brimmed hat to protect you from the sun.

Blackberries: pick when the berries are jet black, very plump and bursting with juice. They will not ripen after picking. Avoid any with red colouring. If the bush has thorns, the berries will be tarter than berries from a thornless bush, but better for cooking.

Blueberries: pick them when they are plump and powdery blue/grey in colour. They won't ripen once picked, so only collect them when they are ready to eat. If a berry shows any red, it isn't ripe.

Elderberries: pick in clusters and then strip the berries from the stems when you get home. Pick underripe berries if you plan to make jam.

Gooseberries: once fruits have reached full size, they may be picked in the green stage, or left on the bush to become pinker and sweeter.

Raspberries: ripe fruit should come away from the plant easily. If you have to use any force, the berry is not ripe.

Strawberries: pick plump, small, firm, red berries without any green or white. Don't overfill the container. When strawberries are packed any higher than five inches deep, the bottom fruits become bruised.

If you plan to keep the fruit for a few days, pick in the early morning or on a cool day. Keep them refrigerated when you get home and only wash them when you are ready to eat, otherwise they will become mushy.

CHAPTER 46

How to Care For Your Teeth

Brush at least twice daily with fluoride toothpaste, after breakfast and before going to bed. If possible, brush after lunch or after eating a sweet snack.

Don't use too much toothpaste. Squeeze out a blob the size of a pea (don't copy people in toothpaste adverts – they use too much – which is what toothpaste manufacturers want you to do, so you will buy more).

Brush all of your teeth, your tongue and gently along the gum line.

Take your time. Set an egg timer and allow three minutes for brushing. Don't stop until all the sand has reached the bottom of the vial.

\#

SCRUBBING
TOO HARD
WEARS THE
ENAMEL
AND CAUS-
ES THE
GUMS TO
RECEDE.

Use a brush with soft bristles. Synthetic bristles are
better than natural ones, because natural bristles are
more porous and can harbour harmful bacteria.
Replace your brush every three months.

Ensure the brush is the correct size – small is best.
Use dental floss and interdental cleaners to get rid of
decay-causing bacteria that brushing alone cannot
remove from between the teeth and under the gum
line.

Place the brush at a 45-degree angle to the tooth surface. Use a short, back-and-forth brushing action to
clean the outside and inside of the teeth and the
chewing surfaces. Tilt the brush vertically and use an
up-and-down brushing action to clean the inside of
the front teeth and gums. Don't forget your back
molars. Brush gently, away from your gums.
Scrubbing too hard wears the enamel and causes the
gums to recede.

Spit out the toothpaste; don't swallow.

Visit the dentist twice a year; s/he will check for cavi-
ties and healthy gums, clean away build up of tartar
and check whether or not you are brushing correctly
by using a special mouthwash that shows up areas
that you have neglected.

Tooth Lore
Women of childbearing age beware: you lose a tooth
for every child.

Chewing fresh blackberry leaves is an ancient cure
for bleeding gums.

If you bite your tongue, someone is speaking about
you behind your back although it might mean you
are going to kiss a fool.

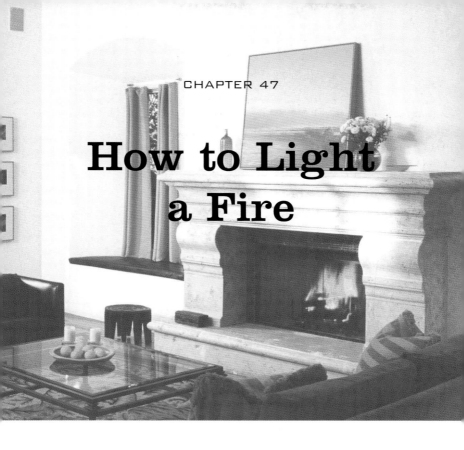

CHAPTER 47

How to Light a Fire

Ensure that your chimney is clean. A dirty chimney will not create the updraft necessary to make a fire burn well.

Clean out the old ashes from the hearth. Starting a fire from scratch is best, because you need to allow plenty of air to circulate; old ashes can stop this from happening.

# #

Lay kin-
dling
sticks in
two lay-
ers, criss-
crossing
on top of
the paper

Screw up about 20 sheets of broadsheet newspaper (avoid using tabloids, as you need more of them and they do not create as much height). Do not scrunch the paper too tightly – imagine you are making meringues – fluffy light balls are best. Make sure that the paper level slopes down slightly towards the back of the hearth.

Lay kindling sticks in two layers, criss-crossing on top of the paper. Ensure that some of the sticks protrude an inch or so beyond the grate, so that when the paper has burned, the grate can provide support and prevent the structure from collapsing.

Now place three medium-sized dry logs vertically on top of the sticks, with the tops resting against the back wall of the fireplace. This will ensure that the flames can catch a maximum surface area.

Place about 15 medium-sized lumps of coal carefully around the base of the logs.

Light the fire and then leave it alone. Add more logs and coal only when it is well established. Adding more material too soon will deprive the fire of oxygen and cause it to smoulder rather than roar.

If the fire fails to catch and you are left with a smouldering ruin, hold a sheet of broadsheet newspaper at the top and place across the mouth of the fireplace. This will increase the draw of air, and levels of oxygen reaching the fire. Keep the newspaper in place even after flames have started to appear. If you remove the sheet too soon, the fire will return to a state of smoking apology. Be vigilant – if the paper begins to brown then it is about to catch fire, and you must place it in the fire.

CHAPTER 48

Live Long and Prosper

If the head of your bed is placed towards the north, you will have a short life; if it is placed to the south, you will have a long life.

On the wedding night, the spouse who falls asleep first will be the first to die.

Carry or wear an acorn to bring luck and ensure a long life.

Passing a young child through the branches of a maple tree will ensure it has a long life.

One's life is prolonged if, in later years, a visit is made to one's place of birth.

On average, right-handed people live nine years longer than left handers.

On Halloween, peel an apple; the longer the unbroken apple peel, the longer your life will be.

The presence of storks should be encouraged; they bring good luck, large families and longevity.

When a baby is being baptised, if it holds its head up it will have a long life; if it holds its head down, its life will be short.

A child will live to old age if it is born within 24 hours of the new moon.

The ancient herb fennel conveys strength, courage and longevity.

Long life requires rewarding pursuits, a feeling of belonging and knowing that you are useful, no matter what your age. This is the stuff of life.

Look on the bright side and laugh at every opportunity.

Tall people; women with large hips and intelligent people live longer than short, small-hipped and stupid folk.

The ancient Egyptians believed the mushroom to be 'the plant of immortality' and decreed that only royalty were allowed to handle or consume them.

A cold head and warm feet ensure long life.

If a Chinese person gives you a peach, they are wishing you long life.

ON AVER-
AGE, RIGHT-
HANDED
PEOPLE
LIVE NINE
YEARS
LONGER
THAN LEFT
HANDERS.

CHAPTER 49

Love and Marriage

If a woman falls when going upstairs, it is a sign that she will fall in love soon.

It is very lucky for a girl to meet her beloved or to kiss him for the first time beneath a new moon. It means that they will soon be wed and their love will be eternal and never blighted by poverty.

If a woman should hear a cock crow while she is thinking of her lover, it is a sign that an early wedding is likely.

Lovers who wish to remain constant should meet on a hillside, among heather and near a stream; meeting on the seashore is also auspicious.

Lovers should not look together at the new moon through glass, lest it should lead them into quarrelling.

Once a couple are bethrothed, they should not be photographed together, or they will part before the wedding or their marriage will be unhappy.

A woman should not try on her wedding ring before the ceremony because it may result in her engagement being suddenly terminated; when trying on her wedding dress, she should leave an item missing, and wear the complete outfit only on her wedding day.

The bride should avoid the temptation to practise writing her married name before the wedding; it is tempting fate.

If a spider is found on the bridal gown or veil it is a sign that wealth and plenty await the married couple.

On the wedding day, once the groom has started his journey to the church he must not turn back. If he

A bride should not wear a green dress (unless she is Irish).

has forgotten something, he should send the best man to fetch it.

Bridesmaids are dressed the same as the bride because this protects her by confusing evil spirits and thus acts as a decoy.

During the honeymoon, an occasional quarrel is not unlucky – it ensures a harmonious and blithe future. The first gift the bride opens should be the first one she uses.

Whoever's gift is opened third by the bride, will soon have a baby.

It is inauspicious for a woman to marry a man whose surname begins with the same letter as her own: To change the name and not the letter is to change for the worst and not the better.

A bride should not wear a green dress (unless she is Irish). Green on a dress symbolises stains gained from illicit liaisons in grassy fields.

CHAPTER 50

Safety

Always run cold water before hot; if a child accidentally falls in the bath he won't be scalded.

Lightning bolts are thrown by devils. During storms, church bells should be rung to scare them away.

In the theatre, do not whistle or clap on stage, wear green, or say "Macbeth" (always refer to it as the "Scottish Play"). Do not wish an actor good luck; instead say "break a leg".

Never light three candles with one match nor have just three candles burning.

Cover your mouth when you yawn because counting a person's teeth robs them of one year of life for every tooth counted.

Do not mow wet grass with an electric mower.

A neat and well lit home is a safer home.

Don't burn bread because it feeds the devil so he will wait close by your house.

Turn all the handles of your pots inwards, so tiny hands cannot reach them.

Walk three times around a fire on St. Johns Eve, and you will be safe from disease for the rest of the year.

Never kill a sparrow; they carry the souls of the dead.

Float with a rip current or undertow. Do not swim against it.

#

FLOAT WITH
A RIP CUR-
RENT OR
UNDERTOW.
DO NOT
SWIM
AGAINST IT.

If you stumble over a threshold, snap at it to send away the demons.

If not used properly, any heating device can let off a deadly, poisonous gas.

Don't sleep on feather pillows because after a while, a ball of feathers will form under your head; when it makes the shape of a complete circle, you will die.

It is unlucky and dangerous to pass someone, trip or turn on the stairs.

Never leave a chip pan unattended.

Never put a spent match back in a matchbox.

Do not talk on the phone during an electrical storm. Turn off and unplug all electric appliances.

Never set 13 people down to dinner, or one will die within a year.

Do not stare into an animal's eyes, if you look away first it will be bad luck, if the animal looks away first then you have a bad spirit around you.

Never walk underneath a ladder. In the days before gallows, criminals were hung from ladders and their spirits would linger underneath.

Step on a pavement crack, break your mother's back.

When passing a cemetery hold your breath lest you should rouse a spirit and breathe it in.

Index